Solve-the-Problem Mini-Books
FRACTIONS & DECIMALS

12 Math Stories for Real-World Problem Solving

by Nancy Belkov

Editors: Maria L. Chang and Lynne M. Wilson
Cover design: Mina Chen
Interior design: Grafica Inc.
Illustrations: Steliyana Doneva

ISBN: 978-1-338-80457-7
Scholastic Inc., 557 Broadway, New York, NY 10012
Copyright © 2023 by Nancy Belkov
Published by Scholastic Inc. All rights reserved.
Printed in the U.S.A.
First printing, January 2023.

1 2 3 4 5 6 7 8 9 10   40   32 31 30 29 28 27 26 25 24 23

Table of Contents

Introduction:
Why Use Stories at Math Time?

Stories help us make important connections in our lives. Through the engaging, relatable stories in *Solve-the-Problem Mini-Books*, students can connect with characters as they figure out how to solve math problems. The characters model asking questions, taking risks, identifying mistakes and misconceptions, justifying their thinking, and trying out ideas. By observing these characters, students can discover processes that will help them make sense of math concepts and solve problems thoughtfully.

Making sense of problems and persevering in solving them is vital to students' success. This key math standard is the backbone of this book. Research shows the effectiveness of teaching math concepts through problem solving.[1] To employ this approach, challenge students with unfamiliar problems that are within their grasp without telling them how to find an answer. Instead of mandating use of a specific operation or strategy, encourage students to try a variety of approaches and strategies independently. Guide them to apply prior knowledge to find these solution paths. As students work together to share ideas and strategies, provide them with prompts, questions, ideas, and materials to support their learning. This approach helps students develop confidence and make connections among math concepts.

Learning problem-solving skills takes time. Just as reading regularly helps students become better readers, seeing and doing math regularly helps them understand and become more confident with math. Embed problem solving in relatable contextual situations to help students see math around them and apply new skills in daily life. Use the stories in this book to help make the connection between problem solving and concept learning more symbiotic and to help students develop as problem solvers.

What's in This Book?

In this book you'll find 12 mini-books and companion practice pages that focus primarily on fraction and decimal concepts and skills. These give students a problem-solving model and opportunities to apply the representations and strategies demonstrated by the characters.

Each mini-book presents a contextual problem, focusing on one of the different problem types identified by Carpenter, Fennema, Franke, Levi, and Empson.[2] These include finding an unknown result, an unknown change, and an unknown starting number through a variety of operations (addition, subtraction, multiplication, and division). Many students struggle to

---

[1] National Council of Teachers of Mathematics (NCTM). (2010, April 8). *Why Is Teaching With Problem Solving Important to Student Learning?* [Research Brief]

[2] Carpenter, T. P., Fennema, E., Franke, M. L., Levi, L., & Empson, S. B. (2014). *Children's Mathematics: Cognitively Guided Instruction*, Second Edition, Heinemann.

understand these kinds of problems, so exposure to all problem types is important—not just with whole numbers but with fractions as well.

How to Use the Mini-Books

Integrating these materials into your current math curriculum is easy. As you plan lessons, consider whether your students have prior knowledge that will enable them to relate to new strategies and concepts in the stories. If you use a curriculum in which students already engage with the problem structures in this book, you may want to use the materials selectively, revisiting problem-solving situations with which your students struggle. A chart of the problem-solving strategies modeled in each mini-book is provided as part of the answer key at the back of the book.

Each mini-book begins with a situational math problem that the student characters must solve. This is followed by "Think" questions, which are designed to help your students learn to read a problem many times (three times is often optimal) to make sense of three essentials:

1) the situation of the problem
2) the question the problem is asking
3) the important information needed to answer the question

Taking time to answer these fundamental questions helps students learn processes for making sense of math problems throughout their work as problem solvers and should become an automatic part of their problem solving.

Create the mini-book. Make double-sided copies of the mini-book so that page 2 appears directly behind the title page. Stack the pages in order and staple along the left side.

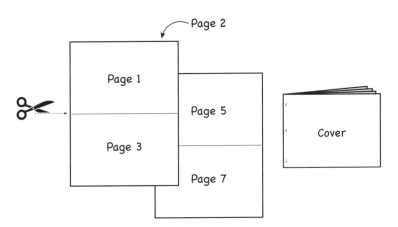

Introduce the mini-book. Students often learn best from other children, so you might introduce a story by saying something like: *Let's see how other students have been solving problems similar to the ones we've been working on.* Project the problem (mini-book page 1) while covering the "Think" questions. Read the problem aloud.

Understand the situation. Uncover the first "Think" question. Successful problem solvers employ a variety of techniques for understanding the problem, including rereading, visualizing, or retelling. Encourage students to try one of the following ways to understand the situation:

- Turn to a partner and describe the situation to each other.
- Draw a picture or diagram to illustrate the situation.
- Act out the situation.

Flexibility with a variety of strategies can help students make sense of problems. Students may use several techniques together or find that one is enough. Facilitate a class share to clarify what is happening in the problem.

Restate the question. Distribute copies of the mini-book. Focusing only on the first page, have students reread the problem and then restate the question in their own words.

Identify the important information. Ask students to identify the information they will need to solve the problem. Discuss why this information is important. Give students the opportunity to think about different ways to use the information, prior knowledge, and modeling tools that might help them solve the problem.

Solve the problem. Students are now ready to think about solution strategies. With some mini-books, you may want students to work in pairs or independently to come up with possible solutions before reading the rest of the story. With others, you may decide to have students move directly to observing how the characters in the story work to solve the problem.

As students read the rest of the story, they will need to process the concepts and strategies the characters use. Whether you use the story as a read-aloud or independent reading, be sure to provide time for discussion and retelling. Encourage students to stop along the way to describe the work the characters do, discuss questions that arise, and try out strategies for themselves. Prompt students to observe how the characters collaborate to solve unfamiliar problems, try out different concepts and strategies, model problems, and reason.

Reflect on the strategies. The last page of each mini-book has "Your Turn" questions to help students analyze the strategies the characters used. These questions provide an opportunity for students to internalize the approaches modeled and clarify underlying math concepts.

Apply the strategies. Finally, use the practice pages to give students the opportunity to try the strategies. These problems encourage students to use at least two problem-solving strategies for each scenario. This promotes self-checking, helps students draw connections, and adds to their tool kits. Have students work independently or in pairs, followed by a class share to address concepts, questions, or struggles.

Animal Race

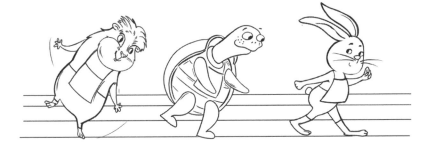

Brianna wrote the following story problem:

A hamster, a rabbit, and a turtle ran a race. When the rabbit reached the finish line, the hamster was only $\frac{3}{8}$ of the way around the track. The turtle was only $\frac{3}{4}$ of the way. After the rabbit, which animal was ahead: the hamster or the turtle?

Mr. Trotter told his students to solve this story problem.

Think

- What is happening in this story?

- What do students need to figure out?

- What is the important information?

1

"Yes, but how can we figure out which animal is next behind the rabbit?" asked Sydney. "The hamster and the turtle each went 3. Did they go the same distance?"

"I don't think so," replied Anthony. "The numerator is 3 for each of them, but the denominators are different. Remember, the numerator just tells how many equal parts we have."

"Okay, each fraction has a different amount of equal parts. Do you think $\frac{3}{4}$ is the smaller fraction since 4 is less than 8?" asked Sydney.

3

"It looks like the turtle and the hamster haven't finished yet. $\frac{3}{8}$ and $\frac{3}{4}$ are less than the whole racecourse," Sydney said to Anthony.

"I agree. The top number is less than the bottom number, so the fraction is less than 1. Look at the fraction chart we made yesterday," Anthony said.

Things We Know About Fractions

- A fraction describes a whole cut into equal parts.

- The bottom number, the denominator, tells how many equal parts are in the whole.

- The top number, the numerator, tells how many equal parts you have.

- If the numerator is smaller than the denominator, the fraction is less than 1.

"Hmm . . . We have to think about how the numerator and the denominator go together. Let's make diagrams of $\frac{3}{4}$ and $\frac{3}{8}$ to see which is less. Let's do $\frac{3}{4}$ for the turtle first," Anthony said.

Anthony drew a rectangle with 4 parts. Sydney drew a circle with 4 parts. She looked at both of their diagrams and wondered why they looked so different.

Solve-the-Problem Mini-Books: Fractions & Decimals © Nancy Belkov, Scholastic Inc. (page 8)

"Our diagrams sure look different," remarked Sydney. "Do you think they both show $\frac{3}{4}$?"

"I don't know. We both made 4 parts in a whole. My parts are equal, but I don't think your parts are equal," said Anthony. "If your circle was a cookie you were sharing, no one would want the small parts on the sides."

"I get it! If I were sharing a cookie with 3 friends, I would cut it in half, then cut the halves in half. That would make 4 equal parts, like this," said Sydney. "I'll shade 3 of the fourths like you did. $\frac{1}{4} + \frac{1}{4} + \frac{1}{4} = \frac{3}{4}$."

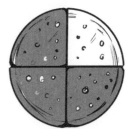

"I'm not sure, but in both of our diagrams $\frac{3}{4}$ is almost the whole thing and $\frac{3}{8}$ is just a little bit. Maybe the size of your diagrams is part of the problem," said Sydney. "Why did you make one rectangle bigger than the other?"

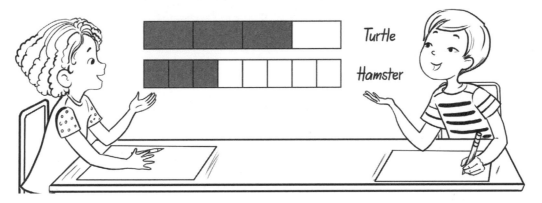

Turtle

Hamster

"You're right! The length of the race was the same for both animals, so both rectangles should be the same," Anthony said. "The wholes need to be the same size for us to compare the fractions. Now, we can see the turtle was closer to the finish line than the hamster."

"Great! Now, let's make diagrams for $\frac{3}{8}$," said Anthony.

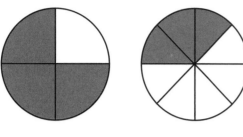

Sydney's Diagrams

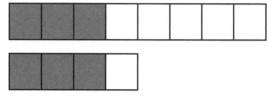

Anthony's Diagrams

"I'm confused. I shaded 3 eighths and 3 fourths, but my diagrams look like the hamster ran the same amount as the turtle," observed Anthony. "Do you know why?"

Your Turn

• How did Anthony and Sydney use diagrams to help them compare $\frac{3}{8}$ and $\frac{3}{4}$?

• Why was it important for Sydney and Anthony to think about the denominators when they compared the fractions?

Solve-the-Problem Mini-Books: Fractions & Decimals © Nancy Belkov, Scholastic Inc. (page 10)

Name: _____

Comparing Fractions

Here are more problems. Try to solve each problem in at least two ways. Think about the strategies Anthony and Sydney used to solve their problem.

1. Paula and Marco made 1-meter-long pieces of paper to make signs for the bulletin board. Paula's pieces were $\frac{1}{5}$ of a meter high. Marco's pieces were $\frac{1}{10}$ of a meter high. Whose pieces were higher?

2. On Monday, Sofia ran $\frac{2}{6}$ of a mile and then walked $\frac{2}{3}$ of a mile. Did she walk or run more on that day?

3. Mr. Trotter bought a pack of 30 large envelopes and a pack of 30 small envelopes so the class could write letters to senior citizens at a nursing home. After the class sent their letters, Mr. Trotter said he had $\frac{2}{3}$ of a pack of small envelopes and $\frac{3}{6}$ of a pack of large envelopes left. Did he have more large envelopes or more small envelopes left?

Solve-the-Problem Mini-Books: Fractions & Decimals © Nancy Belkov, Scholastic Inc. (page 11)

4. Emma and Jamal collect stickers. They each bought two dozen animal stickers at the school store. Emma said $\frac{3}{4}$ of her stickers were birds. Jamal said $\frac{5}{6}$ of his stickers were birds. Which of them bought more bird stickers?

5. Lucas and Maria are reading the same book. Lucas said he has read $\frac{3}{8}$ of the book. Maria said she has read $\frac{9}{10}$ of the book. Who is closer to finishing the book: Lucas or Maria?

Extension: Change the numbers in one of the problems above or make your own problem about comparing fractions. Solve your problem.

Solve-the-Problem Mini-Books: Fractions & Decimals © Nancy Belkov, Scholastic Inc. (page 12)

Missing Measuring Cups

Solve-the-Problem Mini-Books: Fractions & Decimals © Nancy Belkov, Scholastic Inc.

On Saturday, Mr. Trotter baked bread with his children. They could find only two measuring cups: a $\frac{1}{6}$ cup and a $\frac{1}{8}$ cup. Using these, they measured $\frac{1}{2}$ of a cup of milk, $\frac{3}{4}$ of a cup of flour, $\frac{1}{3}$ of a cup of oil, and $\frac{2}{3}$ of a cup of sugar. Mr. Trotter asked his students: *How did my kids measure the milk, flour, oil, and sugar using only those two measuring cups?*

Think

- What is happening in this story?

- What do students need to figure out?

- What is the important information?

1

Solve-the-Problem Mini-Books: Fractions & Decimals © Nancy Belkov, Scholastic Inc. (page 13)

"That gives me an idea. I think they could use the $\frac{1}{8}$ cup to measure the flour," Taylor said.

"How?" asked Hector. "8 is greater than 4. So, wouldn't the $\frac{1}{8}$ cup be bigger than a $\frac{1}{4}$ cup?"

"Think about it. If you divide a rectangle into 8 parts, those parts would be smaller than if you divide that same rectangle into 4 parts," replied Taylor.

$\frac{1}{4}$	$\frac{1}{4}$	$\frac{1}{4}$	$\frac{1}{4}$

$\frac{1}{8}$	$\frac{1}{8}$	$\frac{1}{8}$	$\frac{1}{8}$	$\frac{1}{8}$	$\frac{1}{8}$	$\frac{1}{8}$	$\frac{1}{8}$

Fourths are larger than eighths.

3

"This sounds tricky. I don't think they had the measuring cups they needed to measure $\frac{1}{2}$ of a cup and $\frac{3}{4}$ of a cup," said Taylor.

"I agree. If they had a $\frac{1}{4}$ measuring cup, then they could easily measure $\frac{3}{4}$ of a cup of flour," said Hector. "A whole cup has 4 fourths, like in my diagram. I shaded 3 of the fourths to show they could use a $\frac{1}{4}$ cup 3 times to measure the flour. $\frac{1}{4} + \frac{1}{4} + \frac{1}{4} = \frac{3}{4}$."

"I get it. So you're saying when the denominator is smaller the parts are larger, like this," observed Hector.

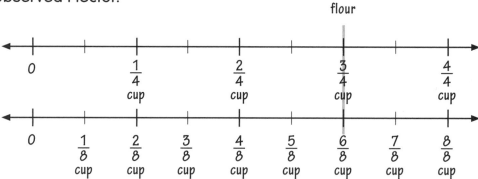

"Exactly! The top number line has 4 equal spaces, and 3 of the spaces show how much flour they needed. The bottom number line has 8 equal spaces. To see how many eighths equal 3 fourths, you double the parts, since 2 × 4 = 8," explained Taylor. "So, I double 3 and I double 4 and see that $\frac{3}{4} = \frac{6}{8}$. I think they used the $\frac{1}{8}$ cup 6 times to measure $\frac{3}{4}$ of a cup of flour."

Solve-the-Problem Mini-Books: Fractions & Decimals © Nancy Belkov, Scholastic Inc. (page 14)

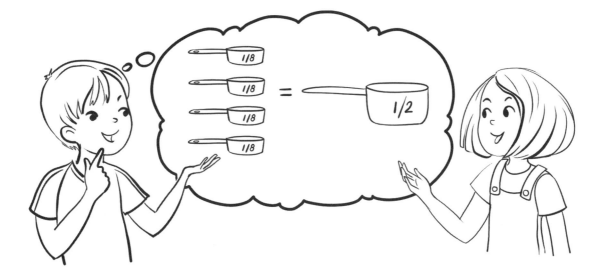

"You're right!" exclaimed Hector. "They also must have used the $\frac{1}{8}$ cup 4 times to measure $\frac{1}{2}$ of a cup of milk. On your number lines, $\frac{2}{4}$ is half of the whole cup and $\frac{4}{8} = \frac{2}{4}$.

"Yes, we showed that $\frac{4}{8} = \frac{1}{2}$ and that $\frac{6}{8} = \frac{3}{4}$. Let's use diagrams and number lines to figure out how they measured the oil and sugar," said Taylor.

"That helps," said Taylor. "If we jumped from 0 to each mark all the way to 1, we would make 6 jumps. But if we skip over a line each time, we make the cup into thirds, like this."

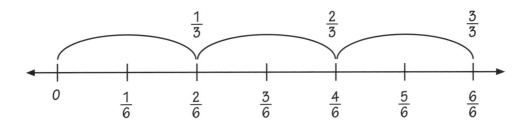

"Yes! That means they must have used the $\frac{1}{6}$ cup 2 times to measure $\frac{1}{3}$ of a cup of oil. So, $\frac{2}{6} = \frac{1}{3}$. How many times do you think they used the $\frac{1}{6}$ cup to measure $\frac{2}{3}$ of a cup of sugar?" asked Hector.

"I'm guessing they used the $\frac{1}{6}$ cup to measure $\frac{1}{3}$ of a cup of oil and $\frac{2}{3}$ of a cup of sugar," said Hector. "The denominator 6 is 2 times the denominator 3. If you divide a whole cup into 6 equal parts, each part would be half the size of each third. Let me show you on a number line with 6 equal parts."

Your Turn

- How many times do you think Mr. Trotter's children used the $\frac{1}{6}$ cup to measure $\frac{2}{3}$ of a cup of sugar?

- How did Hector and Taylor use diagrams and number lines to help them figure out how to use the $\frac{1}{8}$ cup and the $\frac{1}{6}$ cup to make the measurements?

- How did thinking about doubles and halves help Hector and Taylor solve their problem?

Name: _____

Finding Equivalent Fractions

Here are more problems. Try to solve each problem in at least two ways. Think about the strategies Hector and Taylor used to solve their problem.

1. Mr. Trotter asked Alexis to read $\frac{1}{2}$ of the chapters in her book. The book had 6 chapters. How many sixths of the book did Mr. Trotter ask Alexis to read?

2. Kevin said he lived $\frac{1}{5}$ of a kilometer from school. Mr. Trotter asked him how many tenths of a kilometer were equal to $\frac{1}{5}$ of a kilometer. How many tenths of a kilometer does Kevin live from school?

3. Izaak and Sydney baked muffins. They wanted to measure $\frac{1}{4}$ of a cup of raisins, but they only had a $\frac{1}{8}$ measuring cup. How can they use the $\frac{1}{8}$ cup to measure $\frac{1}{4}$ of a cup of raisins?

4. Tiana said she ran $\frac{2}{3}$ of a mile after school. Nia ran $\frac{5}{9}$ of a mile after school. Mr. Trotter asked Tiana to figure out how many ninths of a mile she ran to help her compare $\frac{2}{3}$ and $\frac{5}{9}$. How many ninths of a mile did Tiana run?

5. Sofia said she ate the same fraction of an apple as her brother. Her brother ate $\frac{4}{5}$ of an apple. How many tenths of an apple did Sofia eat?

6. Find at least three equivalent fractions for $\frac{1}{2}$.

Extension: Change the numbers in one of the problems above or make your own problem about equivalent fractions. Solve your problem.

Solve-the-Problem Mini-Books: Fractions & Decimals © Nancy Belkov, Scholastic Inc. (page 18)

The Most Popular Pet

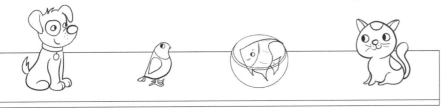

Mr. Trotter's students conducted a class survey about house pets. They found out that:

- $\frac{4}{8}$ of the students had fish
- $\frac{5}{8}$ had dogs
- $\frac{3}{4}$ had cats
- $\frac{1}{4}$ had birds
- $\frac{1}{6}$ had no pets

There are 24 students in all. (Note: Some students had more than one type of pet.) Mr. Trotter asked his class to rank the pets from the least popular to the most popular.

Think

- What is happening in this story?
- What do students need to figure out?
- What is the important information?

1

"Me, too. I think diagrams will help us. I made a diagram of 24 circles for all the students. Since 24 ÷ 6 = 4, I made 6 equal columns with 4 bubbles in each column. Each column is a sixth," said Jayla.

"OK. Since $\frac{1}{6}$ of our classmates don't have pets, they would fill one of your six columns," said Izaak.

"And one row of 6 circles is $\frac{1}{4}$ of the class," said Jayla. "Looking at both diagrams, I see that $\frac{1}{6} < \frac{1}{4}$. I think when the numerators are the same, the fraction with the larger denominator is the smaller fraction."

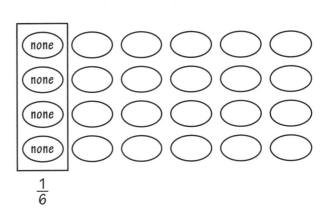

"I'm surprised to see so many kinds of pets," Izaak said to Jayla. "I thought everyone just had a dog like me. I read that dogs are the most popular pet in our country."

"Well, $\frac{5}{8}$ of us have dogs, and 5 and 8 are large numbers. But I think we need to see how the numerator and denominator in each fraction go together to see which fraction is greatest," said Jayla.

"Yes, you're right," said Izaak. "Let's compare $\frac{1}{4}$ and $\frac{1}{6}$ first. Fractions with 1 in the numerator are easier for me to understand."

"I agree. And look: $\frac{3}{4}$ of the class is more students than $\frac{1}{4}$ of the class. $\frac{3}{4}$ is 3 of the 4 equal rows, and $\frac{1}{4}$ is only 1," observed Izaak. "Does that mean when the denominators are the same, the fraction with the smaller numerator is the smaller fraction?"

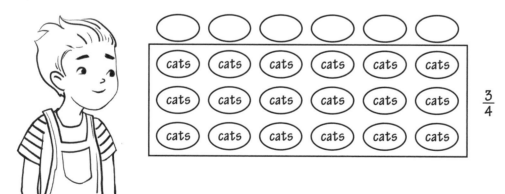

$\frac{3}{4}$

"I think so," replied Jayla. "When the denominators are the same, you have the same size parts. So the fraction with the larger numerator has more of those parts. Let's put $\frac{1}{4}$, $\frac{1}{6}$, and $\frac{3}{4}$ on a number line to compare how popular all the pets are."

Solve-the-Problem Mini-Books: Fractions & Decimals © Nancy Belkov, Scholastic Inc. (page 20)

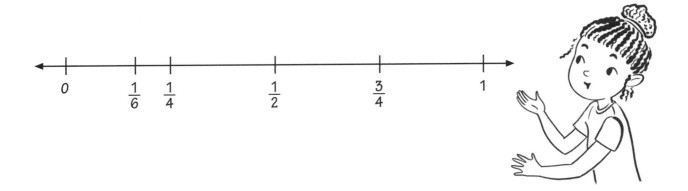

"Why did you put $\frac{1}{2}$ and 1 on your number line?" asked Izaak. "Those numbers aren't on our list."

"1 is for our whole class, and 0 is for none of us. I put $\frac{1}{2}$ on the line because it is halfway between 0 and 1. That helps me figure out where the other fractions go. I know $\frac{1}{6}$ and $\frac{1}{4}$ are less than $\frac{1}{2}$, and $\frac{3}{4}$ is right between $\frac{1}{2}$ and 1," replied Jayla.

"That makes sense since $\frac{1}{2} = \frac{2}{4}$, and $1 = \frac{4}{4}$," said Izaak. "I think I know where $\frac{4}{8}$ goes. Since 4 is half of 8, $\frac{4}{8} = \frac{1}{2}$, right?"

"I agree since $\frac{5}{8}$ is $\frac{1}{8}$ less than $\frac{6}{8}$, and $\frac{6}{8} = \frac{3}{4}$," said Jayla. "I made an array of circles to be sure. Each row is $\frac{1}{4}$ of the whole. I cut each row in half to make 8 equal parts. So, $\frac{2}{8} = \frac{1}{4}$. And 6 of the 8 parts is the same as 3 of the 4 equal parts."

"Now I'm sure that $\frac{3}{4} > \frac{5}{8}$. That means that more of us have cats than dogs. I'm surprised," said Izaak. "Let's survey the whole school to see if we get the same results."

Solve-the-Problem Mini-Books: Fractions & Decimals © Nancy Belkov, Scholastic Inc. (page 21)

"Right! This diagram also shows that $\frac{4}{8} = \frac{1}{2}$. If we divide 24 students into 8 equal parts, there are 3 students in each part. So, $\frac{1}{8}$ of the class is 3 students. And we can see that $\frac{4}{8}$ is the same as $\frac{1}{2}$," said Jayla.

$$\frac{4}{8} = \frac{1}{2}$$

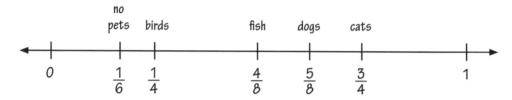

"Let's write $\frac{4}{8}$ on our number line instead of $\frac{1}{2}$," suggested Izaak. "So $\frac{4}{8} > \frac{1}{4}$ and $\frac{4}{8} < \frac{3}{4}$. We can put $\frac{5}{8}$ on the number line too. It is $\frac{1}{8}$ more than $\frac{4}{8}$. But I think $\frac{5}{8} < \frac{3}{4}$."

Pets in Our Class

no pets	birds		fish	dogs	cats	
0	$\frac{1}{6}$	$\frac{1}{4}$	$\frac{4}{8}$	$\frac{5}{8}$	$\frac{3}{4}$	1

6

Your Turn

• How did Jayla and Izaak use diagrams to help them compare all the fractions?

• How did Jayla and Izaak use their understanding of numerators and denominators to help them compare fractions?

8

Name: _____

Ordering Fractions

Here are more problems. Try to solve each problem in at least two ways. Think about the strategies Jayla and Izaak used to solve their problem.

1. Tiana surveyed her class to find out what kinds of chores her classmates do at home. She found out that $\frac{2}{4}$ of her classmates helped do the laundry, $\frac{2}{3}$ fed their pets, and $\frac{2}{8}$ helped cook dinner. Which chore do most of her classmates do? Which chore do they do the least?

2. Thomas bought pint bottles of red, blue, and yellow paint. He used them to paint a gift for his family. When he was finished, he had $\frac{2}{6}$ of a pint of blue paint left, $\frac{5}{6}$ of a pint of red paint left, and $\frac{4}{8}$ of a pint of blue paint left. Which color bottle had the most paint left? Which had the least?

3. One week Anthony kept track of how much he practiced playing his recorder each night. Some nights he practiced $\frac{4}{6}$ of an hour, some nights he practiced $\frac{1}{12}$ of an hour, and other nights he practiced $\frac{6}{12}$ of an hour. What were the longest and the shortest amounts of time that he practiced that week?

4. Kayla surveyed her class to find out which sports her classmates liked. She found that $\frac{7}{8}$ of the class like to run, $\frac{2}{8}$ like to play tennis, $\frac{2}{6}$ like to play softball, and $\frac{2}{4}$ like to swim. Put the sports in order from the most popular to the least popular.

Extension: Change the numbers in one of the problems above or make your own problem about ordering fractions. Solve your problem.

Solve-the-Problem Mini-Books: Fractions & Decimals © Nancy Belkov, Scholastic Inc. • page 24

Who's Read the Most?

Solve-the-Problem Mini-Books: Fractions & Decimals © Nancy Belkov, Scholastic Inc.

Five students in a book group were reading the same book. They divided the book into equal sections to help them figure out what fraction of the book each of them has read so far. Mr. Trotter put their fractions in a list:

$$\frac{7}{8}, \ \frac{5}{6}, \ \frac{4}{10}, \ \frac{3}{5}, \ \frac{4}{5}$$

He asked his class to compare the fractions to see which students were furthest along in the book.

Think

- What is happening in this story?
- What do students need to figure out?
- What is the important information?

1

"Okay, but the fractions $\frac{7}{8}$, $\frac{5}{6}$, $\frac{4}{10}$, $\frac{3}{5}$, and $\frac{4}{5}$ look so different. They will be tricky to compare," said Hailey. "I do see two fractions with the same denominators: $\frac{4}{5}$ and $\frac{3}{5}$."

Hailey drew a rectangle and divided it into 5 equal sections.

$\frac{1}{5}$	$\frac{1}{5}$	$\frac{1}{5}$	$\frac{1}{5}$	$\frac{1}{5}$

"That's a good place to start. Let's compare the numerators to see how many of the 5 sections those two students have read," said Kevin. "The person who read $\frac{4}{5}$ has read more than the person who has read $\frac{3}{5}$, since 4 > 3. So, $\frac{3}{5} < \frac{4}{5}$. I'll start a list of the comparisons."

Solve-the-Problem Mini-Books: Fractions & Decimals © Nancy Belkov, Scholastic Inc. (page 25)

"Does Mr. Trotter want us to figure out when they will each finish the book?" Hailey asked Kevin.

"I don't think we have enough information to figure that out," replied Kevin. "We only know what fraction of the book each one has read so far. Mr. Trotter wants us to compare how much of the book each student has read."

"I think $\frac{4}{5} > \frac{4}{10}$. Their numerators are both 4, so those students each read 4 of their sections. But the person who read $\frac{4}{10}$ read 4 smaller sections, and the person who read $\frac{4}{5}$ read 4 longer sections," said Hailey.

$\frac{1}{5}$	$\frac{1}{5}$	$\frac{1}{5}$	$\frac{1}{5}$	$\frac{1}{5}$

$\frac{1}{10}$	$\frac{1}{10}$	$\frac{1}{10}$	$\frac{1}{10}$	$\frac{1}{10}$	$\frac{1}{10}$	$\frac{1}{10}$	$\frac{1}{10}$	$\frac{1}{10}$	$\frac{1}{10}$

"I agree," said Kevin. "Now, let's compare $\frac{4}{10}$ and $\frac{3}{5}$. My diagram shows that $\frac{2}{10} = \frac{1}{5}$, so $\frac{4}{10}$ of the book equals $\frac{2}{5}$. Since $\frac{2}{5}$ is less than $\frac{3}{5}$, $\frac{4}{10} < \frac{3}{5}$. The person who read $\frac{4}{10}$ of the book read less than the person who read $\frac{3}{5}$. $\frac{4}{10}$ is less than half of the book."

"How do you know that $\frac{4}{10}$ is less than $\frac{1}{2}$?" asked Hailey.

"Well, $\frac{5}{10}$ is 5 of 10 equal parts, so $\frac{5}{10}$ is half of a whole. That's more than 4 tenths," replied Kevin. "I understand fractions better when I figure out if they are more than or less than $\frac{1}{2}$."

"I like that strategy. So, the students who read $\frac{3}{5}$ and $\frac{4}{5}$ of the book read more than half of the book since 3 and 4 are both more than half of 5. The person who read $\frac{4}{10}$ of the book read less than half. So, $\frac{4}{10} < \frac{4}{5}$ and $\frac{4}{10} < \frac{3}{5}$," said Hailey.

"Yes, eighths are smaller than sixths," said Hailey. "If you only have 6 equal parts in a whole, they are bigger than eighths. So, $\frac{7}{8}$ is closer to 1 whole than $\frac{5}{6}$ is."

$\frac{1}{6}$	$\frac{1}{6}$	$\frac{1}{6}$	$\frac{1}{6}$	$\frac{1}{6}$	$\frac{1}{6}$

$\frac{1}{8}$	$\frac{1}{8}$	$\frac{1}{8}$	$\frac{1}{8}$	$\frac{1}{8}$	$\frac{1}{8}$	$\frac{1}{8}$	$\frac{1}{8}$

"Yes. And $\frac{5}{6}$ is closer to 1 whole than $\frac{4}{5}$, since fifths are bigger than sixths. As the denominator gets smaller, the pieces get larger. So, $\frac{1}{5} > \frac{1}{6}$ and $\frac{4}{5} < \frac{5}{6}$," said Kevin.

"Looks like the person who read $\frac{7}{8}$ is closest to finishing the book, and the person who read $\frac{4}{10}$ has the most reading left to do," said Hailey.

Solve-the-Problem Mini-Books: Fractions & Decimals © Nancy Belkov, Scholastic Inc. (page 27)

"The student who read $\frac{5}{6}$ of the book also read more than half of the book. 3 is half of 6, so $\frac{5}{6}$ is more than half. Maybe $\frac{5}{6}$ is the largest of the fractions," said Kevin.

"Or maybe it's $\frac{7}{8}$," replied Hailey. "It's more than half too. Half of 8 is 4 and $\frac{7}{8} > \frac{4}{8}$. In fact, it's almost the whole book, since there is only $\frac{1}{8}$ left for that person to read."

"Good point. The person who read $\frac{5}{6}$ of the book only has 1 part left to read too, but that part is a sixth, not an eighth. Won't that help us compare $\frac{7}{8}$ and $\frac{5}{6}$?" asked Kevin.

6

Your Turn

- What is the order of the fractions from largest to smallest?

- How did Kevin and Hailey use what they knew about numerators and denominators to help them compare fractions?

- How did Kevin and Hailey use the benchmarks $\frac{1}{2}$ and 1 to help them put the fractions in order?

Solve-the-Problem Mini-Books: Fractions, Fractions, Fractions & Decimals © Marcy Rolley, Scholastic Inc. Inage 001

Name: _____

Ordering Fractions

Here are more problems. Try to solve each problem in at least two ways. Think about the strategies Kevin and Hailey used to solve their problem.

1. Nia surveyed her classmates to find out what kinds of jobs they might want to have in the future. Many students chose more than one answer.

- $\frac{4}{10}$ chose firefighter
- $\frac{1}{6}$ chose postal worker
- $\frac{3}{5}$ chose lawyer
- $\frac{4}{5}$ chose doctor
- $\frac{5}{6}$ chose teacher

Order the job choices from least popular to most popular.

2. Sammy made five collages with different colored paper tiles. He figured out what fraction of each collage was made of red paper tiles.

- Collage One: $\frac{11}{12}$
- Collage Two: $\frac{2}{5}$
- Collage Three: $\frac{4}{5}$
- Collage Four: $\frac{5}{10}$
- Collage Five: $\frac{5}{6}$

Order the collages from the one with the highest fraction of red paper tiles to the one that had the lowest.

3. Owen asked his friends how long they read every night. Grady said he reads for $\frac{4}{6}$ of an hour, Brianna said she reads for $\frac{1}{2}$ of an hour, Michael said he reads for $\frac{3}{12}$ of an hour, and Carla said she reads for $\frac{3}{4}$ of an hour. Put Owen's friends in order of most to least time spent reading every night.

4. Hector used reasoning to put a list of fractions in order. He thought about the size of each fraction and compared them to benchmarks. He checked the order by drawing diagrams or number lines. Pretend you are Hector and put these fractions in order from least to greatest: $\frac{3}{7}$, $\frac{8}{9}$, $\frac{1}{7}$, $\frac{13}{14}$, $\frac{5}{8}$, $\frac{3}{14}$.

Extension: Change the numbers in one of the problems above or make your own problem about ordering fractions. Solve your problem.

Ordering Garden Seeds

- What is happening in this story?

- What do students need to figure out?

- What is the important information?

Mr. Trotter's class was looking at seeds for their garden. They noticed that the packet of celery seeds weighed 0.35 grams and the packet of cucumber seeds weighed 0.7 grams. Mr. Trotter asked his students: *Why aren't the packets the same weight? Which one is heavier?*

1

"Yes, but the packet weighs 0.35 grams not 35 grams," replied Kayla. "The 35 comes after the decimal point. So, 0.35 grams and 0.7 grams are both less than 1.0, which is a whole gram. For whole numbers, the number is on the left side of the decimal point. I think that 0.7 > 0.35, but I can't explain why."

"I wish 0.7 and 0.35 were written as fractions with numerators and denominators. I understand fractions written that way," said Michael.

"I wonder if the heavier packet has more seeds," Michael said to Kayla.

"Maybe. But maybe the seeds in the heavier packet are just bigger, heavier seeds," said Kayla.

"You may be right," said Michael. "I think the packet of celery seeds is heavier because it weighs 0.35 grams. We know that 35 > 7."

"That's a great idea! Let's write 0.7 and 0.35 as fractions," said Kayla. "I think the denominator is 10 for 0.7. It's all about place value. The decimal point helps us keep track of the value of the places. The numbers on the right of the decimal point are parts of a whole. The first digit is in the tenths place, like this square divided into 10 parts."

$\frac{1}{10}$ or 0.1	$\frac{1}{10}$ or 0.1	$\frac{1}{10}$ or 0.1	$\frac{1}{10}$ or 0.1	$\frac{1}{10}$ or 0.1	$\frac{1}{10}$ or 0.1	$\frac{1}{10}$ or 0.1	$\frac{1}{10}$ or 0.1	$\frac{1}{10}$ or 0.1	$\frac{1}{10}$ or 0.1

"That diagram helps. So, $0.7 = \frac{7}{10}$. We can color seven of the tenths to show 0.7. It's 0.1 + 0.1 + 0.1 + 0.1 + 0.1 + 0.1 + 0.1. Now, how do we write 0.35 as a fraction?" asked Michael.

Solving-the-Problem Mini-Books: Fractions & Decimals © Nancy Belkov, Scholastic Inc. (page 32)

"Let's look at this place value chart for help. You can see the decimal and the ones place. To the left of the ones place is the tens place, which is 10 × 1. To its left is the hundreds place, which is 10 × 10 × 1," explained Kayla. "The place on the right of the decimal point is a tenth, which is $\frac{1}{10}$."

Hundreds	Tens	Ones	.	Tenths	Hundredths
$10 \times 10 \times 1$ $= 100 \times 1$	10×1	1×1		$\frac{1}{10}$	$\frac{1}{10} \times \frac{1}{10}$ $= \frac{1}{100}$

"I see. So after the tenths come the hundredths, a whole divided by 10 × 10. That is the same as $\frac{1}{100}$. So, 0.35 = $\frac{35}{100}$," said Michael. "I divided our square into hundredths. Let's color 35 of the tiny squares one color. We can keep coloring with a different color until we get to 70. That makes it easy to see that 0.35 is less than 0.70."

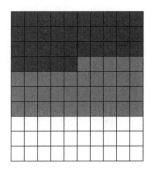

"That made it easy to see that 0.7 > 0.35 because 70 hundredths is more than 35 hundredths," remarked Michael. "The packet of cucumber seeds weighs 70 parts of a whole gram, while the packet of celery seeds weighs 35 parts of a whole gram."

"I can picture the seeds inside a cucumber. I'm sure they're bigger than the tiny celery seeds my mom gets in a jar," said Kayla. "That must be why the packet of cucumber seeds is heavier."

"We can also compare decimals on open number lines," suggested Kayla. "I'm sure 0.7 > 0.5 since $\frac{7}{10}$ is 2 more tenths than $\frac{5}{10}$. It's also closer to 0.5 than to 1.0 since 0.7 is 0.3 away from 1.0."

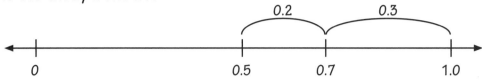

"Let's use the benchmarks $\frac{1}{2}$ and 1 to see where $\frac{35}{100}$ belongs. For 100 parts, the halfway point is $\frac{50}{100}$. That's more than $\frac{35}{100}$. I think 0.35 is 0.15 before 0.50 since 15 + 35 = 50 in whole numbers," said Michael.

"0.7 = 0.70, so let's put 0.70 on the number line. Since 20 + 50 = 70, we know that 0.70 is 0.20 away from 0.50," said Kayla.

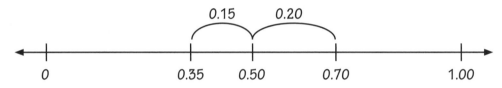

Your Turn

• On page 5, why did Michael color 70 small squares to show 0.70?

• How did Kayla and Michael use diagrams and number lines to help them compare decimal fractions?

Solve-the-Problem Mini-Books: Fractions & Decimals © Nancy Belkov, Scholastic Inc. (page 34)

Name: _____

Comparing Decimals

Here are more problems. Try to solve each problem in at least two ways. Think about the strategies Kayla and Michael used to solve their problem.

1. Jamal walked 0.6 kilometers to school, and Lola walked 0.8 kilometers to school. Who had a longer walk to school?

2. Daniel and his dad bought two packs of vegetable seeds for their home garden. The pack of carrot seeds weighed 0.75 grams. The pack of lettuce seeds weighed 0.48 grams. Which pack was heavier?

3. Emma put her two favorite stuffed animals in her backpack. The rabbit weighs 0.4 grams, and the frog weighs 0.12 grams. Which one is lighter?

4. Taylor used 0.09 meters of red ribbon and 0.2 meters of blue ribbon for an art project. Did Taylor use more red ribbon or more blue ribbon?

5. Sofia had a muffin recipe that called for 0.37 grams of oats. Sammy's recipe called for 0.5 grams of oats. Whose recipe called for more oats?

Extension: Change the numbers in one of the problems above or make your own problem about comparing decimal fractions. Solve your problem.

Solve-the-Problem Mini-Books: Fractions & Decimals © Nancy Belkov, Scholastic Inc. (page 36)

Framed!

Mr. Trotter wanted to make a frame for the class photo. He had a special 1-meter-long strip of wood. The class picture measures $\frac{2}{10}$ of a meter high and $\frac{24}{100}$ of a meter long. He asked the class to figure out if his strip of wood was long enough to make a frame for the picture.

Think

• What is happening in this story?

• What do students need to figure out?

• What is the important information?

1

"Let's make a diagram of the frame. That will help me figure it out," said Carla.

"Good idea," said Thomas. "Here's a rectangle with two opposite sides that each measure $\frac{2}{10}$ of a meter. The other opposite sides need to be $\frac{24}{100}$ of a meter each. I think that means that those sides are longer than $\frac{2}{10}$ of a meter, but I'm not sure."

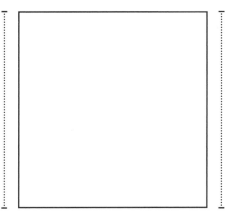

$\frac{2}{10}$ meter

$\frac{2}{10}$ meter

3

"How can Mr. Trotter use one long strip of wood to go around a photo with four sides?" Carla asked Thomas.

"He'll cut the strip into four pieces, one for each side," replied Thomas. "We need to figure out if the 1-meter strip is long enough to go all the way around."

"I think $\frac{24}{100} > \frac{2}{10}$, too. To be sure, let's write both of the fractions as decimal fractions. We can write them both as hundredths. Doesn't $\frac{24}{100} = 0.24$ and $\frac{2}{10} = 0.20$?" asked Carla.

"I'm sure $\frac{24}{100} = 0.24$," replied Thomas. "But let's check to see if $\frac{2}{10} = 0.20$. I drew a number line showing a meter. Then I made 10 sections for the tenths. I marked 0.2 on the line."

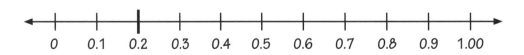

0   0.1   0.2   0.3   0.4   0.5   0.6   0.7   0.8   0.9   1.00

Solve-the-Problem Mini-Books: Fractions & Decimals © Nancy Belkov Scholastic Inc. (page 38)

"Let's find 0.2 on this number line that Mr. Trotter gave us. It shows each tenth divided into 10 parts. 10 × 10 = 100 parts," said Carla.

0   0.10   0.20   0.30   0.40   0.50   0.60   0.70   0.80   0.90   1.00

"When I look at both of our number lines, I see that 0.2 is the same distance from zero as 0.20. So, $0.2 = 0.20 = \frac{20}{100}$," observed Thomas. "If I go 4 spaces to its right, I get to 0.24, and $0.24 = \frac{24}{100}$. So, you are right that $\frac{24}{100} > \frac{2}{10}$. I'll write the measurements in the diagram as hundredths."

5

"I have another strategy," said Carla. "First I add $\frac{24}{100}$ plus $\frac{24}{100}$ to get $\frac{48}{100}$. Then, I add $\frac{2}{10}$ plus $\frac{2}{10}$ and get $\frac{4}{10}$. Since $\frac{2}{10} = \frac{20}{100}$, I know that $\frac{4}{10} = \frac{40}{100}$. These equations show another way to find the perimeter."

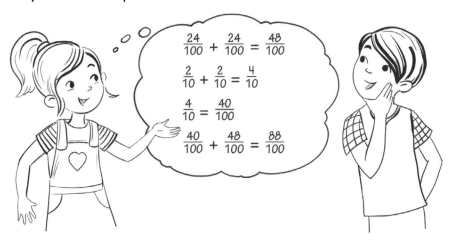

$$\frac{24}{100} + \frac{24}{100} = \frac{48}{100}$$
$$\frac{2}{10} + \frac{2}{10} = \frac{4}{10}$$
$$\frac{4}{10} = \frac{40}{100}$$
$$\frac{40}{100} + \frac{48}{100} = \frac{88}{100}$$

"Great, now I'm sure we are right. Let's tell Mr. Trotter his strip of wood is long enough to make the photo frame. He'll be so happy," said Thomas.

Solve-the-Problem Mini-Books: Fractions & Decimals © Nancy Belkov, Scholastic Inc. (page 39)

"So Mr. Trotter needs at least $\frac{20}{100} + \frac{20}{100} + \frac{24}{100} + \frac{24}{100}$ of a meter of wood for the frame," said Carla.

"Yes," replied Thomas. "If we add the two heights to the two lengths, we get the frame's perimeter."

"Since all the fractions are hundredths, we can just add all the numerators," said Carla.

"Good idea. That's like (20 + 20) + (24 + 24), or 40 + 48 = 88," said Thomas. "Except the addends are hundredths, so the perimeter is $\frac{40}{100} + \frac{48}{100}$, which equals $\frac{88}{100}$. That is almost $\frac{90}{100}$ on the number line. It is less than 1 meter."

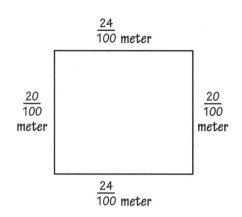

$\frac{24}{100}$ meter

$\frac{20}{100}$ meter

$\frac{20}{100}$ meter

$\frac{24}{100}$ meter

Your Turn

• How did Thomas and Carla use drawings and number lines to help them understand what Mr. Trotter needed for the frame?

• How did Thomas and Carla use the length and height measurements to figure out the perimeter of the photo?

Solve-the-Problem Mini-Books: Fractions & Decimals © Nancy Belkov, Scholastic Inc. (page 40)

Name: _____

Adding Tenths & Hundredths

Here are more problems. Try to solve each problem in at least two ways. Think about the strategies Thomas and Carla used to solve their problem.

1. Jayla kept her dry dog food in a large can. It contained 0.25 kilograms of dry food. Then she found another open bag of dry dog food. It weighed 0.14 kilograms. Jayla added that food to the can. How many kilograms of dog food does she have in the can now?

2. Nia and Daniel made a 2-meter-long poster. It was divided into two sections. The top section was $\frac{3}{10}$ of a meter high. The bottom section was $\frac{45}{100}$ of a meter high. How high was their poster?

3. Mr. Trotter wanted his class to figure out the perimeter of their city park. He told the class that the park was 0.15 kilometers long and 0.09 kilometers wide. What is the perimeter of the park?

4. Kevin had $\frac{6}{10}$ of a liter of red paint. He added $\frac{80}{100}$ of a liter of blue paint to his red paint to make purple paint. How many liters of purple paint did he make?

5. Lucas ran $\frac{4}{10}$ of a kilometer more on Tuesday than he ran on Monday. On Monday he ran 0.75 kilometers. How far did he run on Tuesday?

Extension: Change the numbers in one of the problems above or make your own problem about adding tenths and hundredths. Solve your problem.

Solve-the-Problem Mini-Books: Fractions & Decimals © Nancy Belkov, Scholastic Inc. (page 42)

A Painting Project

Mr. Trotter volunteered to paint the playroom in his son's daycare center. He needed one gallon of yellow paint to cover the whole room. Other families donated the paint. Mr. Trotter wrote this problem for his class:

Laila's family gave $\frac{2}{8}$ of a gallon of yellow paint for the playroom. Trevor's family donated $\frac{2}{8}$ of a gallon more paint than Laila's family. Then I found $\frac{3}{8}$ of a gallon of yellow paint in my garage. I need 1 gallon of paint for the project. Do I have enough?

Think

- What is happening in this story?

- What do students need to figure out?

- What is the important information?

1

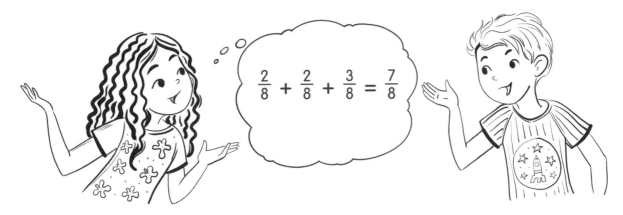

$$\frac{2}{8} + \frac{2}{8} + \frac{3}{8} = \frac{7}{8}$$

"You're right! So, we can add the paint Mr. Trotter found to the paint from Laila's family and from Trevor's family," said Owen.

"I'll add all the amounts together on a number line," said Paula.

"I'll write equations to add the fractions. Mr. Trotter has $\frac{2}{8}$ of a gallon from Laila's family, $\frac{2}{8}$ of a gallon from Trevor's family, and $\frac{3}{8}$ of a gallon that he found. Since all the fractions are eighths of a can, I can just add the numerators. I know that $2 + 2 + 3 = 7$, so $\frac{2}{8} + \frac{2}{8} + \frac{3}{8} = \frac{7}{8}$. That's not a whole gallon," said Owen.

3

"I don't think Mr. Trotter has enough paint, do you?" Owen asked Paula. "His can only has $\frac{3}{8}$ of a gallon of paint in it. If the can had markers to show eighths of a can, it might look like this. Mr. Trotter has $3 \times \frac{1}{8}$ of a gallon, which is not a full gallon."

"Yes, but Laila's and Trevor's families each brought him some paint," replied Paula. "We need to add all the parts of a gallon together."

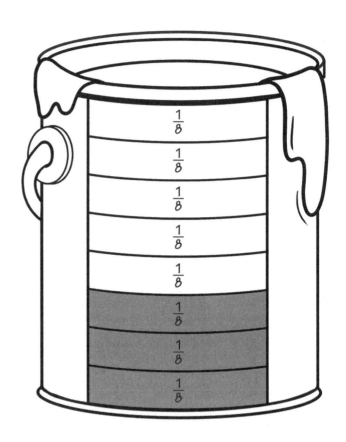

"Yes, $\frac{7}{8}$ isn't 1 gallon. But look at my open number line," Paula said. "I got more than 1 gallon when I put all the parts of cans together."

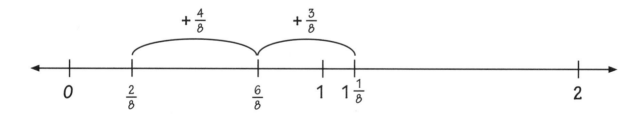

"I see you started at $\frac{2}{8}$, added $\frac{4}{8}$, then added $\frac{3}{8}$. I added $\frac{2}{8} + \frac{2}{8} + \frac{3}{8}$. Where did you get $\frac{4}{8}$ from?" asked Owen.

"The problem says Trevor's family gave Mr. Trotter a can of yellow paint that had $\frac{2}{8}$ gallon *more* than what Laila's family gave," answered Paula. "That means Trevor's family gave $\frac{4}{8}$ gallon of paint, not $\frac{2}{8}$. I had to read that part again to see how much paint Trevor's family gave."

Owen reread the problem. "I get it," he said. "Mr. Trotter got $\frac{2}{8}$ gallon from Laila's family, but $\frac{2}{8}$ gallon *more* from Trevor's family. So, you added $\frac{2}{8} + \frac{2}{8}$ and got $\frac{4}{8}$ gallon of paint."

"Yes, and $\frac{2}{8} + \frac{4}{8} = \frac{6}{8}$. Then I added the $\frac{3}{8}$ gallon that Mr. Trotter found in his garage," said Paula.

"Either way works. So we know that Mr. Trotter has more than 1 gallon of paint, which is more paint than he needs. Now, he just has to paint the room. Do you think he'll do it after school?" Owen asked. "He's a busy man!"

"Did you break apart the $\frac{3}{8}$ into $\frac{2}{8}$ + $\frac{1}{8}$ before adding it to $\frac{6}{8}$?" Owen asked. "I did that on my number line. First, I added $\frac{2}{8}$ to the $\frac{6}{8}$ to make a whole, then I added one more eighth. Did you do that too?"

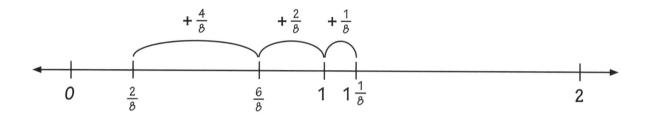

"No. I knew $\frac{6}{8}$ + $\frac{3}{8}$ = $\frac{9}{8}$," replied Paula. "That's the same as $\frac{8}{8}$ + $\frac{1}{8}$ or 1 whole plus 1 extra eighth. So, $\frac{6}{8}$ + $\frac{3}{8}$ = $\frac{11}{8}$."

6

Your Turn

• How did Owen and Paula figure out which fractions to add to see if Mr. Trotter had enough paint?

• What strategies did Owen and Paula use to add the fractions?

Name: _____

Adding Fractions

Here are more problems. Try to solve each problem in at least two ways. Think about the strategies Owen and Paula used to solve their problem.

1. Nolan left home and walked $\frac{1}{5}$ of a kilometer to go to the store. Then he walked $\frac{3}{5}$ of a kilometer to visit his friend. What is the total distance he walked?

2. Trevor's family drinks $\frac{3}{8}$ of a gallon of milk each day. Laila's family drinks $\frac{3}{8}$ of a gallon of milk more than Trevor's family drinks each day. How much milk does Laila's family drink each day?

3. Mr. Trotter bought two bunches of bananas. One bunch weighed $\frac{4}{5}$ of a kilogram. The other bunch weighed $\frac{2}{5}$ of a kilogram. How many kilograms did the two bunches of bananas weigh together?

4. Paula likes to write stories and make them into books. She has inch-long labels for her books. She writes the title on the top section and her name on the bottom section of the label. The bottom section of each label is $\frac{5}{8}$ of an inch high. The top section is $\frac{2}{8}$ of an inch higher than the bottom section. How high is the top section of her book labels?

5. After school Owen helped to clean up the school grounds. He spent $\frac{1}{6}$ of an hour picking up hats and gloves that students lost, $\frac{4}{6}$ of an hour picking up trash and sticks, and $\frac{3}{6}$ of an hour picking up paper for recycling. Did he spend more than an hour cleaning up the school grounds? How do you know?

Extension: Change the numbers in one of the problems above or make your own problem about adding fractions. Solve your problem.

Solve the Problem Mini Books: Fractions & Decimals © Nancy Belkov, Scholastic Inc. Lesson 18

Passing Time on the Train

Trip to the museum tomorrow!

Solve-the-Problem Mini-Books: Fractions & Decimals © Nancy Belkov, Scholastic Inc.

Mr. Trotter's class was getting ready for their train trip to a museum. The trip would take $1\frac{1}{2}$ hours. The students will need to be quiet so they don't disturb other passengers. Mr. Trotter asked his students to plan how they might occupy themselves during the $1\frac{1}{2}$ hour trip.

Think

- What is happening in this story?

- What do students need to figure out?

- What is the important information?

①

"Okay, but I'd rather do a puzzle than play a game on the train," said Jamal.

"We can make doing puzzles one of the choices. Let's make a chart to show some different plans," said Lola.

	Play Game	Eat	Sleep	Do Puzzle	Read
Plan 1			$1\frac{1}{2}$ hours		
Plan 2		$\frac{1}{2}$ hour	1 hour		

"How can we break apart $1\frac{1}{2}$ hours to fit three or four activities?" asked Jamal.

Solve-the-Problem Mini-Books: Fractions & Decimals © Nancy Belkov, Scholastic Inc. (page 44)

"I can sleep for $1\frac{1}{2}$ hours," Jamal said to Lola.

"But there is so much more we can do on the train. I am going to bring a book, a quiet game, and some snacks. I won't have time to sleep," said Lola.

"Well, I can sleep for 1 hour and eat for $\frac{1}{2}$ an hour," said Jamal.

"I hope you'll play a game with me too. Let's list some different possible plans," said Lola.

"Let's start by splitting up the whole hour," replied Lola. "We can spend $\frac{1}{2}$ an hour on each of three different activities. Or we can split up the halves into smaller parts."

"Okay. We can spend $\frac{1}{2}$ an hour on your game, $\frac{1}{2}$ an hour on my puzzles, and then eat for $\frac{1}{2}$ an hour. $\frac{1}{2} + \frac{1}{2} = 1$, and $1 + \frac{1}{2} = 1\frac{1}{2}$," said Jamal.

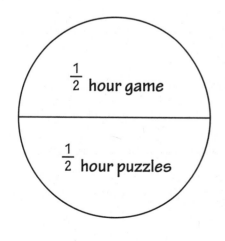

$\frac{1}{2}$ hour game

$\frac{1}{2}$ hour puzzles

$\frac{1}{2}$ hour eating

"I don't think I need $\frac{1}{2}$ an hour for eating. That's 30 minutes. Remember, one hour is 60 minutes," said Lola. "What if we split the whole hour into 4 equal parts? $4 \times 15 = 60$, so a $\frac{1}{4}$ hour is 15 minutes long. In one hour we can spend $\frac{1}{4}$ of an hour on 4 different activities. $\frac{1}{4} + \frac{1}{4} + \frac{1}{4} + \frac{1}{4} = 1$ hour."

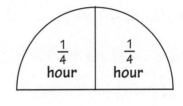

"Don't forget about the other $\frac{1}{2}$ hour. We can also split that into fourths. Your diagram shows that $\frac{1}{4} + \frac{1}{4} = \frac{2}{4}$. That's the same amount as $\frac{1}{2}$ an hour. So, we'll have $\frac{6}{4}$ hours on the train," said Jamal.

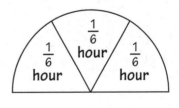

5

"Great! We can even split the time into smaller parts, like sixths, since $6 \times 10 = 60$," explained Lola. "So, we can split up $1\frac{1}{2}$ hours like this."

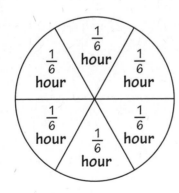

"You're right! We can find all kinds of ways to split up $1\frac{1}{2}$ hours," said Jamal. "We have a good start on this project. I wonder how many more plans we can make."

"That's 6 quarter hours. We only have five activities to choose from. Do we need to think of another activity?" asked Lola.

"I don't think so. Let's put 2 of the quarter hours together and do puzzles for $\frac{2}{4}$ of an hour. That will be really fun. $\frac{1}{4} + \frac{1}{4} + \frac{1}{4} + \frac{1}{4} + \frac{2}{4} = 1\frac{2}{4}$. Now we have two more plans on our chart," said Jamal.

	Play Game	Eat	Sleep	Do Puzzle	Read
Plan 1			$1\frac{1}{2}$ hours		
Plan 2		$\frac{1}{2}$ hour	1 hour		
Plan 3		$\frac{1}{2}$ hour	$\frac{1}{2}$ hour	$\frac{1}{2}$ hour	
Plan 4	$\frac{1}{4}$ hour	$\frac{1}{4}$ hour	$\frac{1}{4}$ hour	$\frac{2}{4}$ hour	$\frac{1}{4}$ hour

Your Turn

- How did Jamal and Lola figure out different ways to split up $1\frac{1}{2}$ hours?

- How did Jamal and Lola use the number of minutes in an hour to decide how many equal parts to make in $1\frac{1}{2}$ hours?

- List three ways to split the $1\frac{1}{2}$ hours using sixths.

Name: _____

Adding Fractions

Here are more problems. Try to solve each problem in at least two ways. Think about the strategies Lola and Jamal used to solve their problem.

1. Grady asked the teachers at his school if they drive to work. $\frac{3}{4}$ of the teachers said they drive all the time, and $\frac{1}{8}$ of the teachers said they drive some of the time. The rest of the teachers said they walk or take public transportation. What fraction of all the teachers said they walk or take public transportation? You might use diagrams of fourths and eighths to help you find the answer.

2. Alexis asked her classmates if they have siblings. She found out that $\frac{2}{3}$ of them have two or more siblings, $\frac{1}{6}$ of them have only one sibling, and the rest don't have any siblings. What fraction of all her classmates don't have any siblings? You might use diagrams of thirds and sixths to help you find the answer.

3. Carla wants to own a pet store where $\frac{1}{2}$ of the animals would be animals with four legs. Some of them could be cats, and some could be dogs. If $\frac{1}{6}$ of all the animals were dogs, what fraction would be cats? Is there another way to combine fractions so that half the animals in the store could be dogs and cats?

4. Marco collects books. He said that $\frac{3}{4}$ of his books are about sports, adventure, and nature. If $\frac{1}{4}$ of his books are about nature, what fractions of his books might be about sports and about adventure? See if you can find more than one answer.

5. Jayla and Hector want to make 1 pound of granola with some oats, nuts, and raisins. What fraction of a pound of each ingredient could they use to make 1 pound of granola? See if you can find more than one answer.

Extension: Change the numbers in one of the problems above or make your own problem about adding fractions to total a given fraction. Solve your problem.

The Walkers

Half of Mr. Trotter's students live less than a mile from school. They walk to school every day, so Mr. Trotter calls them the Walkers. He asked the Walkers to figure out what fraction of a mile each of them walks to school. They put their distances on a line plot.

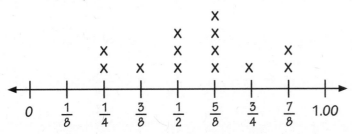

Then Mr. Trotter asked the class: *How much longer is the longest walk than the shortest walk?*

Think

- What is happening in this story?

- What do students need to figure out?

- What is the important information?

1

"You're right. So, we need to find the difference between $\frac{7}{8}$ mile and $\frac{1}{4}$ mile. How do you find the difference between fractions?" asked Daniel.

"I have a strategy for finding the difference with whole numbers that might work with fractions," said Brianna. "When I was 8 and my brother was 10, I figured out the difference between our ages. I asked, how many more years until I am 10? 8 + ? = 10. I used a number line and got 2 years."

3

"It looks like more Walkers live $\frac{5}{8}$ of a mile away from school than any other distance," Brianna said to Daniel.

"And only one person lives $\frac{3}{8}$ of a mile from school," said Daniel.

"One person lives $\frac{3}{4}$ of a mile from school. But Mr. Trotter wants us to compare the longest and shortest walks," said Brianna.

"You added up from the smaller number to the larger number. Let's try adding up from the smallest fraction, $\frac{1}{4}$, to the largest fraction, $\frac{7}{8}$, to find the difference between the longest walk and the shortest walk. Like this," said Daniel.

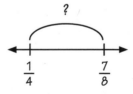

"I wish those fractions were both eighths or fourths of a mile. I can figure out how to get from $\frac{1}{4}$ to $\frac{2}{4}$. But I don't know how to get from $\frac{1}{4}$ to $\frac{7}{8}$," said Brianna.

"That is the challenge! Let's rename one of the fractions. We can see in this diagram that $\frac{1}{4} = \frac{2}{8}$. And $\frac{2}{8}$ has the same denominator as $\frac{7}{8}$. Let's find the difference between $\frac{2}{8}$ and $\frac{7}{8}$ mile," said Daniel.

$\frac{1}{8}$	$\frac{1}{8}$						

$\frac{1}{4}$			

"We can also use the benchmark $\frac{1}{2}$ to find the difference. Our diagrams show that $\frac{1}{2} = \frac{4}{8}$. So I'll jump from $\frac{2}{8}$ to $\frac{4}{8}$ and then jump to $\frac{7}{8}$. Then I add my jumps of $\frac{2}{8}$ and $\frac{3}{8}$, like this," said Brianna.

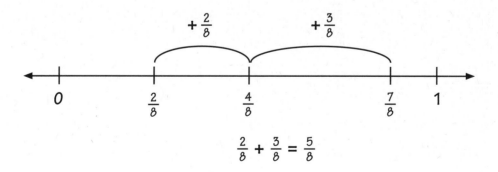

$$\frac{2}{8} + \frac{3}{8} = \frac{5}{8}$$

"I like that. We got the same answer with all of our strategies. So, I'm sure that $\frac{7}{8}$ of a mile is $\frac{5}{8}$ of a mile longer than a $\frac{2}{8}$ of a mile walk. I think our drawings really helped us!" said Daniel.

"Good idea. We can subtract 2 from 7 to find the difference between the numerators. Since 7 – 2 = 5, that means $\frac{7}{8}$ has 5 more eighths than $\frac{2}{8}$ has. If we crossed out 2 of the eighths in $\frac{7}{8}$, we would have $\frac{5}{8}$ left. So $\frac{7}{8} - \frac{2}{8} = \frac{5}{8}$," said Brianna.

$\frac{1}{8}$	$\frac{1}{8}$						

$\frac{1}{8}$	$\frac{1}{8}$	$\frac{1}{8}$	$\frac{1}{8}$	$\frac{1}{8}$	$\frac{1}{8}$	$\frac{1}{8}$	

$\frac{2}{8}$ is $\frac{5}{8}$ smaller than $\frac{7}{8}$.
The difference between the shortest and the longest walk is $\frac{5}{8}$ mile.

"Let's see if we get the same difference if we start at $\frac{2}{8}$ and add up to $\frac{7}{8}$," said Daniel. "To get from 2 to 7, I need 5 more. So to get from $\frac{2}{8}$ to $\frac{7}{8}$, we need $\frac{5}{8}$ more."

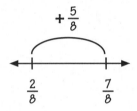

6

Your Turn

• What strategies did Brianna and Daniel use to solve the problem?

• How did Brianna and Daniel use diagrams and number lines to help them work with the fractions?

Name: _____

Finding the Difference

Here are more problems. Try to solve each problem in at least two ways. Think about the strategies Daniel and Brianna used to solve their problem.

1. Jayla had $\frac{5}{6}$ of a bag of dog food. Her neighbor ran out of dog food, so Jayla gave him $\frac{1}{6}$ of the bag. How much of the bag of dog food did Jayla have left?

2. Lucas needed $\frac{7}{8}$ of a cup of butter for a recipe. He could only find $\frac{3}{8}$ of a cup of butter. How much more butter did he need?

3. Marco had $\frac{5}{6}$ of a pack of pencils. He took part of the pack to school. He left $\frac{1}{3}$ of the pack at home. What fraction of the pack did he take to school?

4. Mr. Trotter's students planted flower seeds. The following week they measured the seedlings. The tallest seedling was $\frac{5}{8}$ of an inch. The shortest seedling was $\frac{1}{4}$ of an inch. What is the difference between the tallest seedling and the shortest one?

5. It snowed one day. That evening, three friends measured the height of the snow near each of their homes. Emma measured $\frac{1}{2}$ of a meter of snow, Lucas measured $\frac{3}{5}$ of a meter of snow, and Alexis measured $\frac{2}{10}$ of a meter of snow. What is the difference between the highest and lowest measurements?

Extension: Change the numbers in one of the problems above or make your own problem about subtracting fractions. Solve your problem.

Solve the Problem Mini-Books: Fractions & Decimals © Nancy Belkov, Scholastic Inc. (page 60)

Pencils for Sale

Mr. Trotter bought several packs of rainbow pencils and striped pencils for his class to sell at the school store. Each pack contains a dozen pencils, but the class will sell the pencils individually. At the end of the week, Mr. Trotter checked in to see whether the store still had at least 48 pencils left to sell for the rest of the month. He wrote the following problem for the class to solve:

The store has $1\frac{11}{12}$ packs of striped pencils left. We have $1\frac{5}{12}$ more packs of rainbow pencils than striped pencils. How many packs of pencils does the store have left to sell? Do we have at least 48 pencils?

Think

- What is happening in this story?

- What do students need to figure out?

- What is the important information?

①

"So, we just have to add $1\frac{11}{12} + 1\frac{5}{12}$, right? Let's move a rainbow pencil into the packs of striped pencils," suggested Emma. "Then we add 2 packs of pencils + $1\frac{4}{12}$ packs of pencils, like this."

$1\frac{11}{12} + \frac{1}{12}$ Packs $1\frac{5}{12} + \frac{1}{12}$ Packs

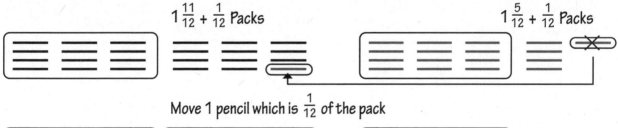

Move 1 pencil which is $\frac{1}{12}$ of the pack

Then add 2 packs plus $1\frac{4}{12}$ packs

"Good idea. It will be easier to add with another full pack and only one partial pack. I can show the addition with these equations," said Grady.

$$1\frac{11}{12} + 1\frac{5}{12} = 1\frac{11}{12} + \left(\frac{1}{12} + 1\frac{4}{12}\right) = \left(1\frac{11}{12} + \frac{1}{12}\right) + 1\frac{4}{12} = 2 + 1\frac{4}{12}$$

③

"There are $1\frac{11}{12}$ packs of striped pencils left. Does that mean the store took one pencil out of a pack of a dozen striped pencils, like this?" Emma asked Grady.

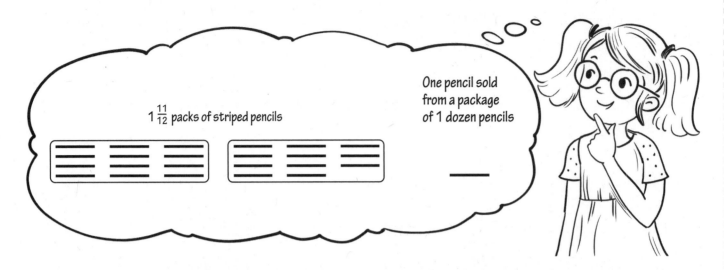

$1\frac{11}{12}$ packs of striped pencils

One pencil sold from a package of 1 dozen pencils

"Yes, we have to figure out if we have at least 48 pencils left. That means 4 packs, since $4 \times 12 = 48$," replied Grady.

"Great! $2 + 1\frac{4}{12} = 3$ packs of a dozen pencils and 4 extra pencils. $3 \times 12 = 36$ and $36 + 4$ more pencils is only 40 pencils," said Emma.

"Mr. Trotter thinks we need at least 48 pencils for the rest of the month. I guess we need to buy more pencils," said Grady.

"Wait a minute. Kayla and Michael just solved the problem and figured out that we have plenty of pencils. Let's read the problem again to see if we made a mistake," said Emma.

Emma and Grady reread the problem.

"I see our mistake," said Grady. "The problem says the store has $1\frac{5}{12}$ *more* packs of rainbow pencils than striped pencils, not just $1\frac{5}{12}$ pencils. So, they have the same amount of rainbow pencils as striped pencils plus $1\frac{5}{12}$ *more* rainbow pencils."

<u>Pencils we have left</u>

| Striped pencils | $1\frac{11}{12}$ packages |
| Rainbow pencils | $1\frac{11}{12}$ packages + $1\frac{5}{12}$ packages |

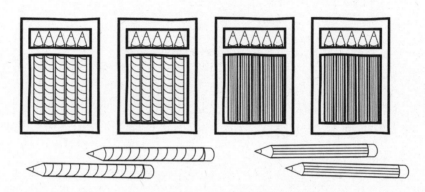

"I agree. We have $\frac{4}{12}$ pack + $\frac{11}{12}$ pack to add to the 4 packs. Let's move $\frac{1}{12}$ from the $\frac{4}{12}$ pack to make the $\frac{11}{12}$ pack into 1 whole pack, then add that pack to the extra $\frac{3}{12}$. $1 + \frac{3}{12} = 1\frac{3}{12}$. We have way more than 48 pencils: $4 + 1\frac{3}{12} = 5\frac{3}{12}$ packs of pencils," said Emma.

$$1 + \frac{11}{12} + 3 + \frac{4}{12} = 1 + 3 + \frac{11}{12} + \frac{4}{12}$$

Add the wholes: $1 + 3 = 4$

Add the partial packs: $\frac{11}{12} + \frac{4}{12} = \left(\frac{11}{12} + \frac{1}{12}\right) + \frac{3}{12} = 1\frac{3}{12}$

Put the wholes with the pencils in the partial packs: $4 + 1\frac{3}{12} = 5\frac{3}{12}$

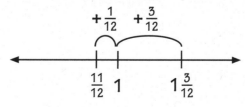

"Great! I hope we get to work at the school store to sell some of those pencils," said Grady.

Solve-the-Problem Mini-Books: Fractions & Decimals © Nancy Belkov, Scholastic Inc. (page 63)

"That was a big mistake. So, we have more rainbow pencils than we thought we had: $1\frac{11}{12} + 1\frac{5}{12}$ packs," said Emma. "We already found that $1\frac{11}{12} + 1\frac{5}{12} = 3\frac{4}{12}$. So now we add the $1\frac{11}{12}$ packs of striped pencils to the total."

After moving 1 rainbow pencil from $1\frac{5}{12}$ packs to $1\frac{11}{12}$ packs

$1\frac{11}{12}$ pack of striped pencils

"Okay, let's add $3\frac{4}{12} + 1\frac{11}{12}$. I'm sure that's more than enough since we have 3 whole packs of rainbow pencils plus 1 whole pack of striped pencils plus extras. The 4 packs alone have 48 pencils," said Grady.

Your Turn

• What mistake did Emma and Grady make in the first half of the story? How did they fix their mistake?

• What strategies did Emma and Grady use to add mixed fractions?

Solve-the-Problem Mini-Books: Fractions & Decimals © Nancy Belkov, Scholastic Inc. (page 64)

Name: _____

Adding & Subtracting Mixed Fractions

Here are more problems. Try to solve each problem in at least two ways. Think about the strategies Emma and Grady used to solve their problem.

1. One day Lucas put books on the class bookshelves. He filled $2\frac{1}{8}$ bookshelves. The next day Sofia put more books on the class bookshelves. She filled $1\frac{3}{8}$ shelves. How many shelves did they fill together?

2. Mr. Trotter got packs of dinosaur pencils for his class to sell at the school store. They sold $1\frac{1}{4}$ packs of the dinosaur pencils in the first day. They sold $3\frac{3}{4}$ packs during the rest of the month. Then they had no more dinosaur pencils to sell. How many packs of dinosaur pencils did Mr. Trotter get at the beginning of the month?

3. Sam ran $1\frac{3}{10}$ kilometers on Tuesday. On Wednesday, he ran $1\frac{5}{10}$ kilometers more than he ran on Tuesday. How many kilometers did Sam run on Wednesday?

4. Nolan and Sofia ran a lemonade stand over the weekend. On Saturday they worked at the stand for $2\frac{5}{6}$ hours. On Sunday they worked for $2\frac{2}{6}$ hours. How many hours did they work at the lemonade stand over the weekend?

5. Lola, Anthony, and Kevin watered the class garden. Lola used $3\frac{3}{4}$ gallons of water, Anthony used $2\frac{1}{4}$ gallons, and Kevin used $2\frac{3}{4}$ gallons. How much water did they use altogether?

Extension: Change the numbers in one of the problems above or make your own problem about adding mixed numbers. Solve your problem.

Building Paper Towers

Mr. Trotter's class worked in pairs to see who could build the tallest tower out of paper and tape. Anthony and Paula made the base of their tower out of short paper cylinders and built the top section using long paper cylinders. Mr. Trotter wrote the following problem about their tower:

Anthony and Paula built a tower that is $5\frac{1}{4}$ feet tall. The top section of their tower is $3\frac{3}{4}$ feet tall. How much taller is the top section than the base of the tower?

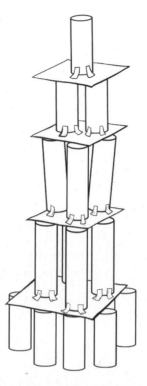

Think

- What is happening in this story?

- What do students need to figure out?

- What is the important information?

①

"Let's read the problem again and draw a diagram to show what we know," said Nia. "That will help us figure out how to solve the problem."

"Okay. The problem tells us the height of the whole tower and the height of the top section. I drew this diagram to show those measurements," said Lucas.

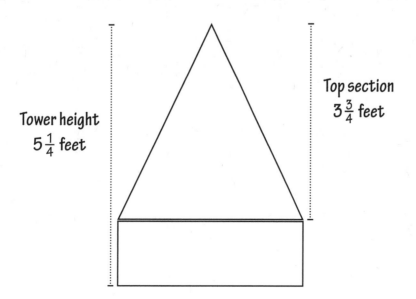

Top section
$3\frac{3}{4}$ feet

Tower height
$5\frac{1}{4}$ feet

③

"I like the tower that Anthony and Paula made. The base looks so sturdy. It looks like it holds the top up very well," Lucas said to Nia.

"Yes, I guess that's how they made it so tall. It's one of the tallest towers in our class," replied Nia.

"Do we know anything else about the tower? What did Mr. Trotter ask us to figure out?" asked Lucas.

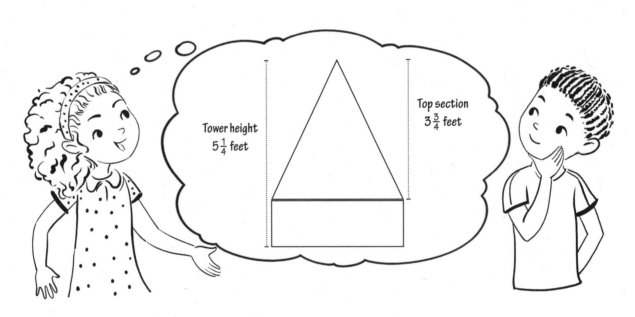

Tower height
$5\frac{1}{4}$ feet

Top section
$3\frac{3}{4}$ feet

"It looks like we don't have the height of the base," observed Nia.

"That's strange. Mr. Trotter asked how much taller the top section is than the base. We need to know the height of the base to compare the heights," said Lucas.

"I agree. So, our first step is to figure out the height of the base," said Nia.

Solve the Problem Mini Books: Fractions & Decimals © Nancy Belkov, Scholastic Inc. (page 68)

"Okay. The height of the base plus the height of the top section must total $5\frac{1}{4}$ inches," said Lucas. "To find the height of the base, let's figure out how much we need to add to $3\frac{3}{4}$ to get up to $5\frac{1}{4}$. First, I'll add $\frac{1}{4}$ of a foot to $3\frac{3}{4}$ to get to 4 feet, since $\frac{3}{4} + \frac{1}{4} = 1$ whole."

$$3\frac{3}{4} + ? = 5\frac{1}{4}$$
$$\frac{3}{4} + \frac{1}{4} = 1, \text{ so} \ldots$$
$$3\frac{3}{4} + \frac{1}{4} = 4$$

"Good start. Let's keep adding up in steps. After adding $\frac{1}{4}$ of a foot to get to 4 feet, let's add another foot to get to 5 feet. Then we just need $\frac{1}{4}$ of a foot more to get to $5\frac{1}{4}$. That's $1\frac{2}{4}$ feet, just like on my number line," said Nia.

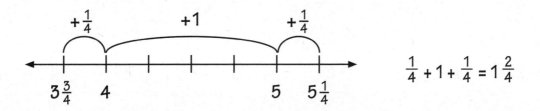

$$\frac{1}{4} + 1 + \frac{1}{4} = 1\frac{2}{4}$$

⑤

"I also got $2\frac{1}{4}$ feet by adding up on this number line," said Nia. "I took three jumps from $1\frac{2}{4}$ to get to $3\frac{3}{4}$ and added the jumps, $\frac{2}{4} + 1 + \frac{3}{4} = 2\frac{1}{4}$. So, the top section is $2\frac{1}{4}$ feet higher than the base."

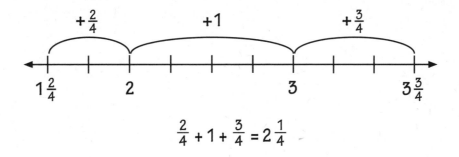

$$\frac{2}{4} + 1 + \frac{3}{4} = 2\frac{1}{4}$$

"Wow, that base must be pretty strong to hold up the tall top section." said Lucas.

⑦

"Wow, the height of the base is much less than the top section," said Lucas.

"Yes, the top section is about 2 feet taller that the base. I just know that the difference between the whole parts of $3\frac{3}{4}$ and $1\frac{2}{4}$ is 2," said Nia.

"Actually, the top section is $2\frac{1}{4}$ feet taller. I compared the $\frac{3}{4}$ and $\frac{2}{4}$ in those mixed numbers. $\frac{3}{4} - \frac{2}{4} = \frac{1}{4}$ since $\frac{2}{4} + \frac{1}{4} = \frac{3}{4}$," said Lucas.

$$3\frac{3}{4} \text{ feet} = 3 + \frac{3}{4} \text{ (top section)}$$

$$1\frac{2}{4} \text{ feet} = 1 + \frac{2}{4} \text{ (base)}$$

$$3 - 1 = 2 \text{ feet}$$

$$\frac{3}{4} - \frac{2}{4} = \frac{1}{4} \text{ of a foot}$$

$$2 \text{ feet} + \frac{1}{4} \text{ of a foot} = 2\frac{1}{4} \text{ feet}$$

6

Your Turn

- How did Nia and Lucas figure out the height of the base of the tower?

- What strategies did Nia and Lucas use to find the difference between the height of the base and the height of the top part of the tower?

8

Solve-the-Problem Mini-Books: Fractions & Decimals © Nancy Belkov, Scholastic Inc. (page 70)

Name: _____

Adding & Subtracting Mixed Fractions

Here are more problems. Try to solve each problem in at least two ways. Think about the strategies Lucas and Nia used to solve their problem.

1. Jamal spent $2\frac{2}{3}$ hours at his grandparents' house. First, he helped his grandparents with chores. Then, they all played card games for $1\frac{1}{3}$ hours. How many hours did Jamal spend helping his grandparents with chores?

2. The path behind Mr. Trotter's house is $1\frac{2}{10}$ meters shorter than the path in the front of his house. The path in front of Mr. Trotter's house is $3\frac{5}{10}$ meters long. How long is the path behind Mr. Trotter's house?

3. Mr. Trotter's class had $2\frac{1}{8}$ pizzas left after a party. Mr. Trotter said that $1\frac{2}{8}$ of the leftover pizzas were sausage and the rest were cheese. He asked his students to figure out how much cheese pizza was left. Draw a diagram. How much cheese pizza was left?

4. Hector's family bought a box of apples that weighed $4\frac{1}{4}$ kilograms. They gave $1\frac{3}{4}$ kilograms of the apples to their neighbors and kept the rest. How many kilograms of apples did they keep?

5. On Monday Lola did jumping jacks for $3\frac{4}{6}$ minutes. She stopped because she was tired. How much longer does Lola need to spend doing jumping jacks on Tuesday in order to increase her time from $3\frac{4}{6}$ minutes to $5\frac{1}{6}$ minutes?

Extension: Change the numbers in one of the problems above or make your own problem about subtracting mixed numbers. Solve your problem.

Timeline Posters

Mr. Trotter's students made timeline posters of their lives from birth to the present day. Kayla claimed her poster was the biggest one since it was 5 feet long. Nolan said his poster was bigger since it was taller than Kayla's. Mr. Trotter asked the class to solve this problem:

Kayla's poster is 5 feet long and $\frac{1}{3}$ of a foot high. Nolan's poster is 3 feet long and $\frac{5}{6}$ of a foot high. Which timeline poster has more square feet?

Think

- What is happening in this story?

- What do students need to figure out?

- What is the important information?

1

"I like the 1-inch squares you drew. I wonder how we can use squares to show the area of the posters. They are only a fraction of a foot high," said Tiana.

"And I wonder why Kayla's poster is only $\frac{1}{3}$ of a foot high. That's the same as 4 inches since $\frac{1}{3}$ of 12 inches is 4 inches," said Sammy. "That doesn't seem like enough space for illustrations and captions."

3

"Kayla's poster is so much longer than Nolan's poster. Doesn't that mean that her poster is bigger?" Sammy asked Tiana.

"Maybe, but I'm not sure," replied Tiana. "The question asks which poster has more square feet. So, Mr. Trotter wants to know which poster covers more area. We need to think about the length *and* the width. Do you remember when we multiplied the length times the height to find the area of different rectangles?"

"Yes. The area of a rectangle that is 2 inches high and 4 inches long is 8 square inches, like this," said Sammy.

"I also wonder what the area of the posters will be when we multiply whole numbers by fractions. Suppose your 2-by-4 inch rectangle was only $\frac{1}{2}$ inch by 4 inches. Wouldn't it shrink?" asked Tiana.

"I think it would. Look at this," said Sammy.

4 inches

2 inches

$\frac{1}{2}$ inch   2 square inches

4 inches

"So, the area is smaller when we multiply a whole number by a fraction instead of by a whole number. When you multiplied $4 \times \frac{1}{2}$, each of the 4 squares was cut in half," said Tiana.

Solve-the-Problem Mini-Books: Fractions & Decimals © Nancy Belkov, Scholastic Inc. (page 74)

"Maybe the area of Kayla's poster is less than the area of Nolan's poster," said Sammy. "For Nolan's poster we multiply $\frac{5}{6}$ × 3. That is almost as much as 1 × 3. But for Kayla's poster, we multiply $\frac{1}{3}$ × 5. It is much less than 5 because $\frac{1}{3}$ is so small."

"I think you are right. Let's use diagrams to compare the area of $\frac{5}{6}$ × 3 and $\frac{1}{3}$ × 5. I drew squares to show $\frac{5}{6}$ × 1 and $\frac{1}{3}$ × 1. I divided one square into sixths and shaded 5 of them, almost the whole square. That's $\frac{5}{6}$ × 1. For $\frac{1}{3}$ × 1, I made thirds and shaded just one of them. That's much less than a whole square," said Tiana.

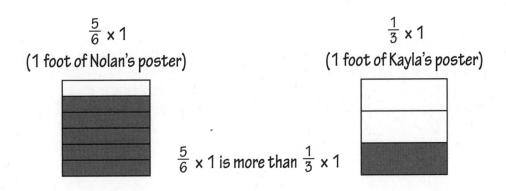

$\frac{5}{6}$ × 1
(1 foot of Nolan's poster)

$\frac{5}{6}$ × 1 is more than $\frac{1}{3}$ × 1

$\frac{1}{3}$ × 1
(1 foot of Kayla's poster)

"I agree. Nolan's $2\frac{3}{6}$ square feet has more shaded space than Kayla's $1\frac{2}{3}$ square feet," said Sammy.

"It's easy to see that the area of Nolan's timeline is more than the area of Kayla's when I stack up 3 × $\frac{5}{6}$ next to 5 × $\frac{1}{3}$," said Tiana.

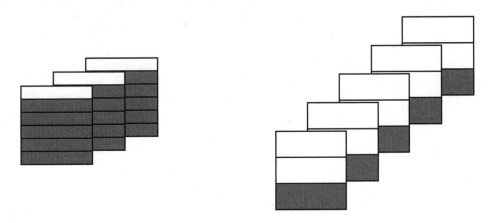

"Yes, it is. I really wonder how Kayla fit captions and illustrations on her poster since it's only 4 inches high," said Sammy.

"Great. The area of Kayla's poster equals 5 of the thirds you drew, or $\frac{5}{3}$. $\frac{5}{3} = \frac{3}{3} + \frac{2}{3}$, which equals $1\frac{2}{3}$," said Sammy.

"And the area of Nolan's poster equals 3 of the $\frac{5}{6}$-foot sections I drew. That is $3 \times \frac{5}{6}$ or $\frac{15}{6}$. Since $15 = 6 + 6 + 3$, $\frac{15}{6} = \frac{6}{6} + \frac{6}{6} + \frac{3}{6}$, which is $2\frac{3}{6}$. $2\frac{3}{6} > 1\frac{2}{3}$," said Tiana.

Area of Nolan's poster is $\frac{5}{6} \times 3$ feet

Area of Kayla's poster is $\frac{1}{3} \times 5$ feet

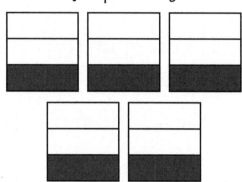

Your Turn

- Why did Sammy and Tiana predict that the area of Kayla's poster was less than the area of Nolan's?

- What strategies did Sammy and Tiana use to find the area of each of the posters?

Name: _____

Multiplying a Whole Number by a Fraction

Here are more problems. Try to solve each problem in at least two ways. Think about the strategies Tiana and Sammy used to solve their problem.

1. Izaak has 6 big notebooks to put on his shelf. Each notebook is $\frac{1}{4}$ of a foot wide. How wide are all the notebooks together?

2. Sofia drinks 2 liters of liquid on days she races. On days when she doesn't race, she usually drinks $\frac{5}{8}$ of that amount. How much liquid does she usually drink on days when she doesn't race?

3. Kevin and Emma picked carrots from their garden. They put the carrots in bags and gave them to their neighbors. They gave out 3 bags of carrots. Each bag weighed $\frac{2}{3}$ of a pound. How many pounds of carrots did they give to neighbors?

4. Grady's timeline poster was 7 feet long. He thought it was too long, so he cut out some parts of it. Then it was $\frac{6}{10}$ of the size it had been. How long was the poster after he cut out some parts?

5. Michael was making bookmarks for presents. He made each bookmark 6 inches long and $\frac{7}{8}$ of an inch wide. What was the area of each bookmark?

Extension: Change the numbers in one of the problems above or make your own problem about multiplying a whole number by a fraction. Solve your problem.

Answer Key

Title	Answers	Strategies include:
Animal Race (Comparing Fractions), *pp. 11–12*	**1.** Paula's (1/5 > 1/10) **2.** walked (2/3 > 2/6) **3.** small (2/3 > 3/6) **4.** Jamal (5/6 > 3/4) **5.** Maria (9/10 > 3/8)	• Draw same-size diagrams of each fraction • Draw area models with a given number of equal parts in each whole and shade given amount of parts • Use relationship of the parts to the whole in each fraction • Decompose fractions into unit fractions • Determine that a smaller denominator indicates a greater fraction when numerators are equal
Missing Measuring Cups (Finding Equivalent Fractions), *pp. 17–18*	**1.** 3/6 of the book **2.** 2/10 km **3.** They can use the 1/8 cup two times because 2/8 = 1/4. **4.** 6/9 of a mile **5.** 8/10 of an apple **6.** Answers may include 2/4, 3/6, 4/8, etc.	• Draw same-size diagrams of each fraction • Decompose fractions into unit fractions • Draw area models or number lines with a given number of equal parts in each whole and indicate a given number of parts • Halve or double amounts of parts in a fraction • Use area models or number lines lined up to show equivalence
The Most Popular Pet (Ordering Fractions), *pp. 23–24*	**1.** feed their pets; help cook dinner (2/3 > 2/4 > 2/8) **2.** red; blue (5/6 > 4/8 > 2/6) **3.** longest 4/6; shortest 1/12 **4.** running, swimming, softball, tennis (7/8 > 2/4 > 2/6 > 2/8)	• Draw area models or number lines with a given number of equal parts in each whole and indicate a given number of parts • Determine that a smaller denominator indicates a greater fraction when numerators are equal • Determine that a larger numerator indicates a larger fraction when denominators are equal • Determine which fractions are equal to, more than, or less than 1/2
Who's Read the Most? (Ordering Fractions), *pp. 29–30*	**1.** Postal worker, firefighter, lawyer, doctor, teacher (1/6 < 4/10 < 3/5 < 4/5 < 5/6) **2.** One, Five, Three, Four, Two (11/12 > 5/6 > 4/5 > 5/10 > 2/5) **3.** Carla, Grady, Brianna, Michael (3/4 > 4/6 > 1/2 > 3/12) **4.** 1/7, 3/14, 3/7, 5/8, 8/9, 13/14	• Draw area models or number lines with a given number of equal parts in each whole and indicate a given number of parts • Decompose fractions into unit fractions • Determine that a smaller denominator indicates a greater fraction when numerators are equal • Determine that a smaller numerator indicates a smaller fraction when denominators are equal • Determine which fractions are equal to, more than, or less than 1/2 • Determine which fraction is closest to a benchmark (0, 1/2, or 1)
Ordering Garden Seeds (Comparing Decimals), *pp. 35–36*	**1.** Lola (0.8 > 0.6) **2.** the carrot seeds (0.75 > 0.48) **3.** the frog (0.12 < 0.4) **4.** blue (0.2 > 0.09) **5.** Sammy's (0.5 > 0.37)	• Use place value to determine the part to whole relationship • Rename decimal fractions as equivalent fractions • Rename decimal fractions in tenths as hundredths • Decompose a decimal into decimal fractions • Represent decimal fractions on area models or number lines • Determine which decimal is closest to a benchmark (0, 1/2, or 1)
Framed! (Adding Tenths & Hundredths), *pp. 41–42*	**1.** 0.39 (39/100) kg **2.** 0.75 (75/100) m **3.** 0.48 (48/100) km **4.** 1.4 (1 40/100) liters **5.** 1.15 (1 15/100) km	• Rename fractions as decimal fractions • Rename decimal fractions in tenths as hundredths • Represent decimal fractions on area models or number lines showing tenths or hundredths • Apply properties used with whole numbers to join and separate parts of same wholes • Add tenths to tenths and hundredths to hundredths • Chunk fractions to make a whole and add remaining fraction to the whole

A Painting Project (Adding Fractions), *pp. 47–48*	**1.** 4/5 of a kilometer **2.** 6/8 of a gallon **3.** 1 1/5 kilograms **4.** 7/8 of an inch **5.** Yes, because 1/6 + 3/6 + 4/6 = 8/6 (or 1 2/6), which is greater than 6/6 (1).	• Add the numerators when denominators are the same • Chunk fractions to add up to a whole, then add any remaining chunks • Rename fractions as a whole and remaining fraction of the whole when the numerator is larger than denominator • Draw area models or number lines to represent and add fractions
Passing Time on the Train (Adding Fractions), *pp. 53–54*	**1.** 1/8 **2.** 1/6 **3.** 2/6; yes (1/8 + 3/8 = 1/2) **4.** Possible answers: 1/4 and 1/4; 1/8 and 3/8 **5.** Possible answers: 1/3 + 1/3 + 1/3; 1/3 + 1/6 + 3/6; 1/4 + 1/4 + 1/2; 1/8+ 3/8 +1/2	• Decompose fractions into unit fractions • Rename fractions to equivalent fractions with the same denominators • Decompose a whole into different combinations of unit fractions • Organize combinations and use one solution to find related solutions • Chunk a fraction into smaller parts • Use area models or number lines to add and to show equivalence • Apply properties used with whole numbers to join and separate parts of same wholes
The Walkers (Finding the Difference), *pp. 59–60*	**1.** 4/6 of a bag **2.** 4/8 of a cup **3.** 3/6 of a pack **4.** 3/8 of an inch **5.** 4/10 of a meter	• Add up from the smaller fraction to the larger fraction • Rename fractions to equivalent fractions with the same denominators • Use area models or number lines to add and to show equivalence • Add or subtract the numerators when denominators are the same • Chunk fractions to add up to friendly numbers • Apply properties used with whole numbers to join and separate parts of same wholes
Pencils for Sale (Adding & Subtracting Mixed Fractions), *pp. 65–66*	**1.** 3 4/8 shelves **2.** 5 packs **3.** 2 8/10 kilometers **4.** 5 1/6 hours **5.** 8 3/4 gallons	• Apply properties used with whole numbers to join and separate parts of same wholes • Use area models or number lines to add and to show equivalence • Chunk fractions to make a whole and add remaining fraction to the whole • Add whole numbers together and fractional parts together, then combine • Use known addition facts • Use equations to represent calculations • Add or subtract the numerators when denominators are the same
Building Paper Towers (Adding & Subtracting Mixed Fractions), *pp. 71–72*	**1.** 1 1/3 hours **2.** 2 3/10 meters **3.** 7/8 of a pizza **4.** 2 2/4 kg **5.** 1 3/6 minutes	• Add up from a smaller fraction to a larger fraction • Add in chunks • Use area models or number lines to add and to show equivalence • Chunk fractions to make a whole and add remaining fraction to the whole • Use equations to represent calculations • Apply properties used with whole numbers to join and separate parts of same wholes
Timeline Posters (Multiplying a Whole Number by a Fraction), *pp. 77–78*	**1.** 6/4 (or 1 2/4) feet **2.** 10/8 (or 1 2/8) liters **3.** 6/3 (or 2) pounds **4.** 42/10 (or 4 2/10) feet **5.** 42/8 (or 5 2/8) inches	• Draw an area model to represent the dimensions of a rectangle with sides that are whole numbers, then shade whole squares and fractional areas • Draw area models to show repeated addition of a whole number by a given fraction • Multiply the given fractions by 1, then add the product the given amount of times • Chunk a mixed number product into a whole number and the remaining fraction